First Edition

No Side Effect
Solutions for
Development
in India

Padmalochan Sahu

Acknowledgement

I am Padmalochan Sahu, student of English literature from India, Odisha. From my Graduation time, I have been planning to write a book for my country's problems. But I write this book after the completion of my M.Phil. Degree. This five years of gaffe give me much more better knowledge on the matters of my country. Before going to write this book, I want to share a little experience which help me to proceed in this writing line. A poor school student who has been suffered from lack of guidance and care. A student who is never liked by any teacher at his school. A student who suffer a lot of family tragedy. A student who see a lot of tragedy of his mother in family. I don't know when and how I get a sharp head and patriotic heart. From my Graduation time I enter into political field both by college Election and by Elective political subject paper. From that time, I get a culture of discussion on various subject matter of our country. After Graduation also I continue to discuss various problems and gradually discussion becomes a regular part of my life. And this discussion culture gives me a sense of solutions in many matters. From discussion I continue to get solutions. Discussion becomes a part of my blood and in these days, I am discussing on many matters with myself. It is the process of continual discussion and deep consideration which brings many solutions.

After discussion culture, I always get a good friend circle to discuss for various problems. I never leave a discussion on country matter that may be argument with my teachers. I cannot remember the name of that friend who once suggested to write my points for my country. I should not forget the name of those friends who always give interest on great discussions; Hitesh, Pinu, Tushar, Sagarika, Aparna and some others. I cannot forget these friends till the last breath of my life.

Contents

Introduction

There are millions of problems in our country India and our government also trying to solve many. But some problems of our country are so serious which are connected with every citizens of our country. There is no lack of intellectuals in our country but there is high lack of patriotic heart and mind which can help to provide real solutions to our country. Many discussions are going in a vulgar manner in our country. Even our Supreme Court never consider deeply to our major problems such as poverty problems, business rules, income matters, corruption matters etc. Now our country's future depends on the various actions of our Governments. I gave the title of this book *No Side Effect Solutions for Development in India* where I try to give solutions for major problems in India which solutions have no side effect. No side effect means no problems will come when India Government will apply these solutions in our country. In many cases, we can find that many riot, movements, fighting and opposes are happen when Government apply some new rule in our country. But I gave the solutions which will not create such problems and will not consume huge money like other programmes of our Government.   I tried to give easiest solutions to the problems.

Many solutions can be made only by psychological changes and for new psychology we must follow some strict rule and we cannot change bad mindset only by request or by T.V advertisement. We cannot claim that hard rules are against Human Right because hard rule are for verdicts or criminals only and only by hard rule we can create a healthy and safety society in our country. Here we don't need to spend huge money to apply strict rule. Govt should not care about few criminals but about billions of people. Saudi Arabia people are enjoying criminal free society and all world admiring it and people from all around the world visiting more and more due to safety system which help a country to earn money. Similarly, our government should not hesitate to apply hard system to clean our country which is also connected with prestige of a country and with earning. Western countries understanding these matters very well and applying into their system and we people are admiring them. No country can prosper by weak rules. Welfare means not weak system and more freedom for criminals and corrupt people. Opposition party never want a Government to be good and to be resultful. Therefore, our Government should not care more about opposition party. Our Government should not do late to apply good and strong system to strengthen our country more and more. Because our sleep will give other country to get chance. Like China getting benefit of our sleep-in productions and other business systems.

But we should not worry more about our development. There are many easy solutions which can bring revolutions in the development of our country. This book is not my last book and I will write more books for my country. In this book I discussed on some major problems with easy solutions such as Agriculture problems, Innovation problems, Start-up problems, Clean less problems, Economic development problems and Education problems. My quest for no side effect solutions will not stop after this book but I will try to search more on this. Because no work or duty greater than duty for country.

A small wrong step will create many problems in future. Decision of India-Pakistan division, Jammu Kasmir by Nehru, Tibet decision by Nehru, many Country policies and Foreign policies are giving us regular problems. Therefore, we should learn from historical mistakes and should give more importance to "No Side Effect" side by which our present and future generations can live their lives without problems.

Chapter 1: Solutions for Agricultural Problems

India is a vast country both by area wise and population wise. Here we cannot find any lack of agricultural land, lack of water, lack of organic fertilizer, lack of farmer, lack of agricultural market, lack of agricultural expert, and lack of many other facilities. It is very sad to hear on the poor and law situations of agriculture with all type of facilities. We need to get the benefit of such huge facilities. We need to get the benefit of perfect agricultural climate in India. With proper guidance and plan for agriculture, we can make the agriculture field more successful than any other country in the world because we have every facility inside our country. By successful agriculture, we can earn billions of dollars from export to foreign countries. In our country we can make many types of agriculture, which most of the countries cannot do due to climate. Every kind of climate and soil are available in our country. We are very strong at organic fertilizer. All these facilities are not available in most of the countries. But we are not getting the benefit of these facilities which is one type of huge hidden economic loss.

To strengthen agricultural field, India Government spending thousands of crores, giving huge amount of loans to farmers with law interest rate, giving subsidies in buying agricultural machines and making agricultural projects, making water facilities in many areas and giving many other facilities to develop and strengthen our agriculture field. Government made thousands of agriculture offices and giving thousands of agriculture officers salary every month. Government giving seeds with cheap prices. But after all, every year many farmers getting suicides, many suffering and are unable to return loan money, many farmers unable to get food properly and many cannot give good educations to their children. Bad situations of farmers can say the condition of agriculture in our country. Therefore we need to find out the problems. On the other hand, we can find many examples of rich farmer in our country but the quantity of those success farmer is very low. So, it become a huge conflict in our country.

Many intellectuals giving solutions regularly. But I want to give a simple process or idea which is so much fit to solve our agricultural problems. Proper use of this idea can bring revolution in agriculture in our country. First of all, now everybody knows it very well that agriculture field is not a small business field in comparison to other businesses. It also can bring an economical revolution in our country. So, our Government should take step for "farmer welfare privatization". In privatization system, Government will give guidelines to private companies by which both farmer and private company can get benefits. Without proper and strict rule, this system will also fade down. Proper management and guidelines can benefit our country.

Since I acquainted more with Odisha, here we can find 8 months of rest of agricultural fields after 4 months of paddy agriculture. People of Odisha giving interest only in paddy agriculture which is not a profitable agriculture at all. But I am not opposing to do that. They can utilize their other 8 month of time with high profitable agriculture such as spices agriculture; ginger, chilli, turmeric, onion, garlic, and other profitable agriculture such as potato, carrot, radish, beat, Kashmiri chilli, bean, corn. Because of shortage of cold-stores, farmer can do agriculture which do not need cold-store such as honey, ginger, chilli (we can make dry red chilli), corn, timber trees (which are used in furniture making), and many agriculture materials which. But our farmers are not adopting diverse kind of profitable agriculture. Similar situations we can find in most of the states in India. There are some issues behind this problem. Farmer have not guts to arrange things in other seasons. They are unable to manage with new agriculture, they are unable to buy machineries and water arrangement elements, they are unable to sell huge amount of goods, they are unable to expert goods to out states and countries. There are many problems inside this matter and for those reason they are not giving interest in valuable or high standard agriculture. Sad news is that we importing billions dollar agricultural material which can be done in India easily.

Now I am discussing the process which India Government can adopt for Agriculture development. Market for agricultural goods are huge in the world. We can sell these goods easily. We can export these with proper system. So we need many Agricultural Trading Companies in India. A private company can invest money in high agricultural system, it can spend money for advance technology, it can make much more production, it can sell goods and make huge money. One can ask how private company will give interest in agriculture sector. Here the role of India Government is so important. Govt. will give every kind of facility to agricultural trading companies. For secure trade, Govt. will make some rule. First, Government will give loan to agricultural trading company with low interest rate i.e. under 3%. Second, Govt. will take minimum GST from these companies. Third, Govt. will provide machineries with proper rate and also can give subsidies to small agriculture companies. Fourth, Govt. will help properly to export goods to other countries. Fifth, Govt. will give quick and easy licence to Agricultural Trading Companies. Sixth, one can get licence with minimum capacity of 3-4 lacks property by which a large number of small companies will come into existence. Seventh, Govt will help to run everything without disputes. After all, here companies will not find land in villages without proper money distribution system. Farmer will not give their land because of some reason. Farmers' lands are situated with small boundary lines so they will never let anyone to destroy their boundary lines. Here Govt. will make strict rule to not to break their boundary lines.

Farmer will not give land without proper payment system so here Govt will make rule for rent system and profit percentage system. One company has to give minimum 30% of profit to farmers. With the guidance of the ATC, farmer will work in field and will get wages also. Here one private company will surely do profitable agriculture which will give profit to farmers for entire year, which will give profit to company and country also. By increasing of agriculture, demand for compost will grow, demand for organic fertilizer will grow, demand for cold stores will grow, demand for waste management and fertilizer making will grow and many other business possibilities will grow. By high production, rate of good will come down and private companies will automatically give focus to export to foreign countries for more profit.

Private companies can use machineries for water facilities which one farmer cannot do. They can use advance system which one farmer cannot do. They can bring export to consult. They can bring hybrid seeds. They can arrange huge selling system. They can do much more things for advance and profitable business. Farmer can give their land for 8 months also because their paddy agriculture in rainy season need 4 months. In this system, Govt will make rule for rent, distribution, wages etc. and will do different fine system for different mistakes. To help companies, Govt. will help to provide security system for protests, for danger, for non-cooperation due to agreement with farmers, for opposition etc. Here Govt. will give strict order to police and to agriculture officers for proper running.

To make this movement success, Govt. will make advertisement. Govt. will make compulsory rule for organic fertilizer usage which will not destroy production capacities of our land in future. Govt. officer will make this movement success. They will talk with local rich people for this system. Govt. will talk with big companies to do this. They will do local advertisement. Govt. will encourage people to open Agricultural Trading Company. Youth will be encouraged to do this with advance system and technologies. It is not difficult task to do. This process will give our country huge economic development and huge employment. Hundreds of farmers from each village will get income. People will get huge income by selling organic compost, by selling compost with waste management systems. By this system, we can be king of Agriculture in world market. But everything all depends on our Government's action. Every facilities are available but action and encouragement waiting to make our country great. By this process, we can bring revolution with short time. This process should be beneficial for both farmers and companies.

Chapter II: Solution for Innovation Problems

As we know that our country India is the second largest population of the world. And we shall be the first population till 2030. Here brain of 130 crore people are running continuously. But it is very sad to hear that we are remaining at the lower level in the Innovation Index of the World. Where is the problem we should find out. We cannot blame Indian people by saying that they are not innovative or they are not giving emphasis to research and innovation. I receive opinion from many people, I discuss with many students and attain many intellectuals' opinion through YouTube videos. After all I consider deeply and finally find out many problems in this field. But they are not so hard to solve.

Before go to deep discussion, I want to discuss various problems in this innovation field. First of all, we cannot find any discussion climate for innovation and research like political discussion and other discussions. Our most of the Indian guardians are discussing on engineering, medical, MBA etc as career and giving emphasis to one and encourage their children for that line as future career. The options of career are so limit for guardians. We cannot ignore the importance of guardians in India. Here we cannot be success without targeting Indian guardians. To create a discussion climate for innovation and research, we should start from guardians and aged people. They are the real energy and back force for many discussions and decisions. Our government making many efforts for advancement for innovation. We can find science exhibition everywhere in India at school level and college level. But the reality is so sad. Most of the school children prepare science projects by the help of their guardians and teachers. They help to make that project but they never give their children real knowledge of innovation and research. Students are preparing their projects by rotting some lines and then presenting. Original innovation is almost impossible to find from there. Here also money investing is result-less. After science exhibition, again they start a life which is out of research and innovation. Again, their guardians start to guide them only for good education and good marks. I just don't understand how a large amount of money investment is not giving any result. How intelligent officers are remaining silent and actionless. How they are not getting original points and problems. Solutions are not hard but all high chair persons and power persons are sitting with hard mentality. They are not observing and thinking for result. They are just going as chief guest and giving their same rotting vulgar speeches which speeches are solutionless and actionless. Second big problem is that our Government is not making any programme like Clean-India to change the mentality of our Indian people. We can start revolution from mentality change. After mentality, other effective steps are necessary. Crore and crore of students are choosing B.Tech line, MBA line, Medical line and here also mentality level working as force. Even B. Tech students are giving no technological innovations and other type of innovations because here "result mentality" of guardians are working as force. School time is the real time of setting mentality in students. Most students are getting mentality of mark competition because of their guardians. Third big problem is our syllabus system which totally unfit for promotion for innovation. There are many mathematics and other educations which have no usage in practical world. We can replace those useless education with useful and promotional education which will help both students and country. Without adoption of "Utilitarian Philosophy" we cannot save our complex and hard future. After all, there are many problems we can find but solution is so simple for me. We can bring a revolution with some little steps and little budgets.

To change mindset of guardians means not to go to them directly and say to leave mark mentality and job mentality. We should target all citizens to change mentality. From study syllabus, we can start this movement. Then our Government can promote this like Clean-India programme. Education will help India more but education should follow utilitarian philosophy. This means not that we should totally ignore moral lessons. Newspapers and news media should be given some order to promote this movement compulsorily. But these are not enough steps to change mind set. One should get simple procedure to do new business. Innovator should get simple procedure to get success. Innovator should get facilities to produce their innovation and our Government also can establish production house for new innovations. They should get high level facilities and security. India Govt. can do this by new rule and here is nothing hard to do. These actions are so much necessary to take.

Is this possible to utilize and train such a huge quantity of brain power in our country? Is this possible for India to be strong in the innovation field? Can our Government can boost innovation quantity by intelligent actions? Is there any system which can give success in innovation field? My answer for above questions is 'yes'. If a small Country like Switzerland can be first in the index of innovation then India can do thousands time better result than Switzerland. Indian can give world record innovations with intelligent facilities. To succeed in innovation field, we do not need to follow policies and systems of Switzerland. We can apply intelligent system according to the situation of our country.

Developmental education and good facilities for innovator are must necessary. I would like to give my personal thought which can bring a revolution in the field of innovation in India. Our Govt. can open a private like organization for innovation programme. This company will give membership to only Indian companies. This company will demand a certain amount of money to give membership. This company will find out innovators of India. This company will find out students who have innovative ideas and will give them facilities to success their ideas. This company will give or sell innovations to only Indian companies which will help India to develop. But innovations will be distributed with a systematic manner to registered companies. But one can ask questions that how quantity of innovations will grow. People always give priority to money and secure career or life. To create a climate of innovation, our Govt. should declare something. First, if any school student will give any innovation or important innovation idea then he/she will get free education for life-time. He/she will get an 30% of selling amount from the company for that innovation. He/she will get a job quota in the company which company will buy that innovation from our Indian Innovation Company of India Government. After all, He/ she will get a scholarship money in every month until 25 years of age. Govt. can categorise to innovations and can give facilities to innovators according to their category. That student also can study research education freely. All these facilities should be declared by advertisement and through different campaign. Every guardian and students will get clear informations on this scheme. After then guardians will surely give importance to innovation field because of above discussed facilities. Most of the guardians will follow this because of "job quota" facility which will give a future security. All the facilities will obviously create a craze in Indian guardians and students. But our Government will also make strict rule for negligence and corruption in this field. Because negligence and corruption will destroy every good system. Hence, it is also a part of important strategy. For corruption and negligence, every employee will give a bond-paper writing for punishment of corruption during joining time. Website facility for complain against negligence and corruption and actions against complained employee will help to succeed this scheme and programme.

This Indian Innovation Company will open an application and website. One student can apply to sell his/her innovation in this website. One student will give a surface idea in this website. Then selected student will be invited to head-office to give presentation of their innovation. Their innovation and idea will be patented for security. Then a selected student will get every above discussed facilities. That student will get the 30% of selling money soon after selling to company and will get a quota for future job in that company. That student also can get free access to research education. Only 100% Indian companies can buy innovation from this company. That company will compulsorily give a job to that innovator and Govt. will decide the minimum salary for that job. Website of Innovation company will give free book to every Indian. This book will give good knowledge on research and guidance to research. Indian people can download this pdf book in every Indian language from that website. This book will help Indian people to get a clear knowledge on research. By this book guardians will get help to guide their children in this field. And students also get good knowledge and get encourage from that book. Not only one book, but also many books will be available on innovation knowledge in every Indian language in this website. People can get books for school level, for college level and for university level. Website should be made in proper and simple manner. People will be encouraged to benefit from this website or application. Govt. will add compulsory research education for every category of students.

Above all, this is not the only solution for innovation problems. There are many but this process is easy and effective. We cannot find any side effect for this process. To success this programme, our Govt. should make private type organisation which will concentrate on effective work without any pressure. Without serious advertisement and without serious actions, this effective process cannot be effective. There is no lack of experts in India and they should be heard by our Govt. to success programmes. Our Govt. should not hesitate to make hard rule for success for this programme. To success in innovation field means to be success in economical development.

Chapter III: Solution for Start-up Problems

Now India is a country of youth or young people. More than 60% of people are young by age that is under 35 years in India. This is a special and revolutionary power. This is the perfect time to bring economic revolution in India. Revolution cannot happen without proper climate and system. Now a huge number of Indian youth are searching for help to do start-up. Many of them will face failure and some may be success. To get benefit of youth power, they should get proper knowledge on business and they should be trained on business world. They should get every facility to success their business. This means not that our Govt. will give money to every interested youth. Facilities means easy access to licence, easy system to import and export, easy process to expert to foreign countries, easy system of market. Our Govt. should try best to provide a proper and easy system to every entrepreneur. Our Govt. should not neglect this opportunity, otherwise our country will lose a large number of business tycoon which is the huge economical loss. Here our Govt. can properly use available source and take some simple steps to success our entrepreneur.

Some days before I went to a bank to ask for start-up loan interest rate and I found that it is 12%. How an entrepreneur will take risk to pay such a high rate of interest. He/she will look for a business settlement for some month and for that they cannot give such a high percent of interest without a proper settlement of business. They need time to settle a business. Second big problem is knowledge on business field. This problem can be solved by our Government by making a website which will give every knowledge on business, Indian business system and law system in every Indian language. At that website one can ask question on business problems and he/she will get answer within short time. One can complain on corruption in that website. Government banks are not checking and observing on an entrepreneur before giving loan. Our Govt. should give this duty to a private company like LIC with terms and conditions. A company will lose tender if that company will make any corruption and negligence and that will face a huge fine also. Start up programme need perfect function and for perfect function, it need privatisation. Because, we all know that negligence is common quality of government officers. A perfect start up programme can change the future of our country and a lose programme can destroy the life of millions of youth.

I think our Government can use technology to success start up problems in our country. In my opinion our Govt. should open a Start-up/ Entrepreneur Application/ Website to solve every kind of Start-up problem. Through this Application, one can get every kind of facilities to get easy access to business field such as one can apply for licence, apply for loan, apply for foreign expert etc. To get start up loan, one has to answer many questions, has to give every demanded document. By satisfy question answer and documents, one can get loan. I want to give some suggestion for important questions: which business you want to do? In which process you will earn money? which plus point of your product can help to sell more than others? Explain your unique points of your business?

Qualification? Address? If you get money then how could you use the money or for which work you will use money? Do you have any experience in any field or any work? Is this an innovative idea or innovation for business? Do you have any machinery facilities? In which area you will sale product and if there any market facilities in that area? Market name and location? Explain in detail the process of profit? How much money you need to success your business? these are the basic important questions which are enough to decide to give loan. The interest rate of start up loan should be less than 3% and for first few months they should give zero interest because of settlement of business. This application should give 100% assurance that their unique idea cannot be shared and hacked and their data information will remain in full secure. After a direct survey to that applicant according to his/her given information, he will get money. But this entire procedure should take less than one month. Here also our government can use Govt. employee for survey and for other helping work. For serious execution to start up plans, our Govt. should create a post of manager or executer in every district.

Except website/application facility, our Govt. should make some strict rule for start-up success. Our Govt. should make some compulsory rule for big companies of India to give venture capital to small local companies of India. Every big revenue companies should invest at least 5- 10 % of perfit money in small start up in India. This process will force small companies of India to grow. Second, our Govt. should make a strict owner system in every company. The founder or starting owner of a company will get the complete control power of his company even after he/she sell all the shares to others. Third, our government should make a rule for foreign investor that they can invest 100% in a company but cannot get the controlling power. Only 80% Indian investment company can get control power over other Indian companies. Our government should make every facilities and securities for venture investors to succeed start up business in India. After all, our Govt. should keep a minimal amount of 10,000 crore for start up and new innovation business for Indian people. Our Govt. can give execution tender to any private company to success these start up plans like private companies who give tender for selling and other executions to other private companies. There should be strict punishment for any kind of negligence in execution.

Chapter IV: Solution for Clean-less Problems in India

Now our India Government giving good effort to make our country clean. Our Government promoting cleanness through different advertisement and campaigns. Our people are also understanding the value of cleanness. But after all these advertisements and campaigns, we can find a huge unclean area in India. Many cities, towns and villages are full of ugly and dirty area. So, our Government should look for practical solutions. It is depending on seriousness of our Government. This clean-less problem can be solved within short time. I am not saying any extra budget for clean problem but proper rule and system can make clean programme success with lower budget. Amount of clean budget of India Government is enough to make our country dirty free. 17,843 crore is enough to clean our country completely. Even we need less money to clean our country with proper system.

There are many solutions for this problem but I want to suggest solutions which can be easier and cheaper without side effects. First, our Government should make some rule for citizens and businessmen for clean India. There should be compulsory dustbin rule for every shop and they should be bound to maintain it. They will keep dustbin in front of their shops. One has to face fine of at least 1000/- in any type of negligence. Fine paper will save shop owner for 5 days only and he/she will face fine punishment if he/she is repeating that problem. One can get 5 days of time to solve his/her dustbin and clean problem after fine punishment.

Here our Government should use police power to success this clean system. Policemen will do patrolling regularly and will check cleanness every where in the market area. They will do fine to any shop owner for negligence in clean system. A shop owner will face same fine punishment if any unclean or dirty areas are found within 2 meters of surrounding area from that shop. Every market complex owner will compulsorily make a lady and a gent's toilet with regular compulsory maintenance. And for other market area, every 20 serial shop owners will make toilet for public and will maintain regularly and this will be compulsory in every market area. Without toilet system, shop owner will lose licence and will also face fine punishment. Checking of cleanness and toilet maintenance will be regular by our policemen. Even policemen will face punishment in the case of negligence. Proper utilization of our police power will make our country cleaner and more success. We have enough quantity of policemen which should be used for success in our country. Similarly, these rules will be compulsory for urban area citizens. Every urban citizens will have to clean the 5-meter front area from his/her home boundary. Here police will firstly pick up the ugly area photo and then will do fine (1000/-) to that home owner. By this rule, every home owner will maintain cleanness to his/her front area. And this process will be success because now in Odisha every biker compulsorily wearing helmet because of police checking and fine system. I myself gave three time fine and after that I always remain afraid to break rule. And now every biker keeping driving licence because of regular police checking and fine system. Similarly, here also people will follow clean rule due to police checking and fine system.

Without strict system, people will always follow negligence and will never take action for cleanness.

Our Government also can make "Decoration Rule" in our country. we can see uncountable number of ugly market place in India. We can also find huge number of poster in scatter way which are making a market ugly looking. We can see shops which are colourless and which are dirty with red pan masala spittle. After clean rule we can see clean area but cannot find good looking area. Therefore, our government should also add some decorative rule for market area and for urban citizens. Our Government can make one compulsory colour (white) maintenance to every shop. One cannot hang poster in an odd manner. One has to compulsorily maintain colour. Government can declare best three decorative shop prizes in every urban market in every year to encourage decoration. Shop owner will get discount in tax also.

For best cleanness, our Government can do privatisation to this field. Privatization can give best result in cleanness. Our government spending thousands of crores to make clean to our areas but we cannot find proper utilization of total money. Here also corruption is the basic problem and negligence is the second big problem. Therefore, our Government should give tender to private companies in every district. Here company will have to do agreement through which company will face fine and punishment in any negligence case. That company will give all waste material to district recycling centre where compost making, bio gas making, electricity production and recycling process will happen. From these process, one district can earn money which money can be used for clean budget inside that district.

Cleanness will give our country benefit from all side. Cleanness and decoration will give our country more foreign visitors which will give income to many people and to our government. Our country will lose the dirty or unclean image for foreign countries. One good thing I would like to share that our Government should not afraid of strict rule for cleanness because people will always find good result from these rules and will always admire for good steps. I always admire to the road safety rules after giving fine also and I hear from many people who admire to the road safety rule of Odisha Government. Rule breaker are few but sufferer are huge. Corrupter are few but sufferer are huge and therefore people will always support for strict rules and good systems. People should see punishment for corruptor and for neglecter by which they will get good hope and believe for Government. After they see action against corruptor, they will obviously support to our Government. One better thing our Government can do that is complaining website for any kind of corruption and negligence and complainer will be unknown. People can upload photos, videos to give prove to any corruption. They can describe in that website with prove. Our Government should also take action against corrupter after complain by which people will get believe for Government and will obviously support for corruption free country.

After all, our government should spend money for proper drainage system, for systematic markets, for planning construction of building, etc. Because big city like Mumbai is suffering for bad water drainage system. One day rain making Mumbai full of water everywhere. Here India Government should make world-class drainage system and water storage system by which farmer can get water in summer day also. These are the perfect area where India Government can invest money for better future of our country.

Chapter V: Solution for Economic Development in India

We can find uncountable merits of India to which we can proudly admire as an Indian. But sad thing is that maximum merits are the given gift of our ancient predecessors. Now we generation are not doing anything which can make our country great in true sense. Even we are unable to follow merits and reputations of our country. But we cannot blame totally, we have organization like ISRO, Ayurveda for which we can feel proud. Our country has millions of problems and our Government cannot solve all those problems. But there are many problems which are connected to millions of people or which are public problems. In my opinion, every problem has simple and intelligent solutions. Among big problems, economical problem is one. Economical process and system of a country decide the food, living and development of all citizens. We are second highest population in the world. A little decision of our Government will affect a huge number of people directly or indirectly. Therefore, economical decisions should be decided after all-round vision. Economical development means not development of GDP but the real development of all citizens. I am not against GDP but supporting all aspect of development. Everything all depend on our Government and policies of our Government. But it is true that maximum problems of our country can be solved in simple manner.

After many effort of our Government, we cannot see a revolutionary economical change like South Korea or like Japan. After Make in India programme also, we cannot find any revolution or change in economy of our country. I would like to start my discussion from Make in India programme. Foreign companies have been getting huge benefits from our country. Therefore, we should not request them to establish factories and manufacturing centre here. Our Government should give order to all foreign companies to establish manufacturing centre compulsorily. Because they are continuously making huge profit from our country and they will obviously follow this compulsory order of our Indian Government. Just recently we see America-Mexico trade deal. We should learn from that agreement. America made some compulsory rule for Mexican companies to do manufacture in America. America also decided the minimum wages of American worker. Similarly, India should make compulsory rule for foreign companies to do manufacture of minimum 70% of selling goods. And car, mobile and other technical companies should compulsorily do 70% manufacture of every device and part of their selling elements. Otherwise one company cannot sale its product. After these rule, every company will get maximum 5 month of time. And then we can obviously find a huge revolution in industrial field. Our Government will also decide the minimum wages of worker per hour. Our Government should not hesitate to do these rules because we are 70 crore people looking for income source. Therefore, decision should be strict and for the sake of citizens' benefit. By these rules also foreign companies will continuously take money from our country. We should not let them exploit freely and comfortably.

One big reason for our economic weakness is our petroleum import. Every year India buying more than 4 lack crores of petroleum from foreign countries which is making our money weaker. So, our Government should make strict decisions to decrease the usage of petroleum. We have many alternative energy sources such as natural gas, solar power, battery power, gober gas etc which can be substitution for petroleum. Battery vehicle can help our country to save money. Thermal battery industry already came to India. Therefore, our Government should give strict order to Indian vehicle companies (TATA, Mahindra, Hero, Bajaj, TVS etc,.) to produce electric vehicle. Our Government can order all companies to make minimum 80% electric vehicle compulsorily. And they cannot make more than 20% of petrol and diesel vehicle. Here also, our Government should give at least 10 months' time to start production. Our Government should give thermal battery technology to every Indian vehicle company with free of cost. Our Government should give order to thermal battery company to make speed manufacturing of thermal battery compulsorily. Our Government can give extra facilities to electric vehicle buyer who will get free accident insurance. Our Government should do advertisement and campaign for making positive impression for electric vehicles. Our Government has to construct many charging points within short time. These are life time investment of our Government which are compulsory need of every time. Rapid work towards this will save huge money of our country and here we can say time is money and time is our source of economical development.

Next big point for our economic development is our agriculture. Only agriculture business has potential to develop our country faster. I already discussed on agricultural development process. I gave a concept of Agriculture Trading Company through which our country can solve agricultural problems properly and effectively.

Tourism also an important part of economical development of a country. India is large country and we have thousands of nature gifted areas but all are not tourist worthy area. We need to utilize many natural beauty areas as tourist destination and we need to decorate them creatively and amazingly. Our country has no lack of talented and creative people. So, we need to do utilize our talented people to strengthen our economic power. Our government can declare for project presentation for a natural place to decorate and the winner will obviously get good money. Other good participants also will get chance to give presentation for other area. After these, we need clean India, decorative India, good foreign policy to increase quantity of foreign tourists. Everything all are available in India to earn money but we need to utilize these properly.

After above problems, we should not forget to discuss on utilization of Government money in various construction projects. Every day we can hear many news of automatic breaking of bridges, breaking of roads which are of huge money, uselessness of big canal and dams etc. By this breaking and uselessness of construction, our country losing thousands crore money every month and every year. These are happening only because of corruption. A construction work starts after giving pocket money to ministers, head officers, Govt. engineers and to local M.P, M.L.A. After satisfying to all these great people, one contractor has to earn profit from that project. Now we can imagine how our bridges, roads are breaking regularly. After breaking problems, we can see many drains are not functioning properly and our towns are remaining ugly out of stock ugly drain water. We can see many dams and canals which remained functionless projects are destroyed huge money from our Government. Corruptions are happening comfortably in these areas. One incident I want to share that one year ago one bridge in Bhubaneswar suddenly break down and 11 people died out of that incident. One of my uncle alleged as a verdict for that incident who is the engineer of that project. Police arrived at his home to arrest him but he was not at home. After some days he returned and stay comfortably at home and after some days he again join at duty. This is the punishment to him for the death of 11 people and for destruction of that over bridge. People and opposition political party blame this incident for two days and Government give assurance for investigation. Investigation will run for 20 years when all verdicts will be old and case may get happy ending for those verdicts. We can learn from Japan, America, South Korea how to give construction tender and how to make strong and useful construction. Punishment for any negligence and crime should be hard and strict. Bell system, case forward system etc are giving courage to corruptors. Government should declare that if any bridge breaking automatically or due to weak work then the contractor of that bridge will give total money to construct that work again. Otherwise Government will cease to all his property including his living home and all lands.

We should not forget to discuss on defence budget of India. I support to huge army budget but I am not supporting to entire dependence on foreign countries. Because we have no lack of talented people, talented students, we should give priority to built world class weapon inside our country. We should produce every little possible thing inside our country. We can get more security with our own built weapons and we can also save exporting money. Depend entirely on other countries is a bad symbol for our economy.

As I told that more dependent on other countries is danger for our economy. We Indians are mostly dependent on China products. Our Government can solve this problem within one year. Our Government should not wait for citizens for production of various things which are not in India and coming from China. Our Government can directly make manufacturing industries by its money. Because Indian Government has no money problem. By producing our own, our Government can save exporting money and can earn money. Indian private companies are unable to make mobile manufacturing company. So, our Government should not wait for this and should make at least one best manufacturing industry which industry can take order from private companies to make any kind of phone. It should have capacity to make every part of a mobile phone. It can take any concept from any private company to make mobile. Similarly, we are not producing any effective doll, technical gadgets. Here also our Government should make a allrounder manufacturing industry which can make any concept and any design to make. If our Government can buy defence machinery, bullet train then it can buy easily production machineries to produce inside country. I am saying for manufacturing industry because now Indian companies have no potential to invest huge money to compete Chinese companies. Even we are unable to produce doll and compete to Chinese companies. Therefore, our Government should take action for these as soon as possible.

Next step to strengthen our economy is the utilization of solar power. We are so fortunate that we born in India but unfortunately, we are not getting the benefit of sun light. Only solar power can fulfil our demanded energy. It is a system of energy that can be used anywhere. Every Indian can use it by personal arrangement without dependence on Government current and electric bill. We should not feel lack of energy in our country. For solar business, I would like to share my personal opinion. This solar business is the big future of earning source. Here our Government should not let free access to foreign companies to exploit. Indian companies have good potential to manufacture solar power objects. By solar power, we can give Indian companies to do free business and we can fulfil energy demand of every

Indian. By this way, our Government can give dual benefit to Indian people. We can fulfil our energy demand until the existence of sun. Therefore, our Government should give priority to cheap solar power elements production in India and by Indians.

Our Government should learn from China Government on creating great business climate. Our Government should do anything for better facilities for businessmen (both for small and big business). Our Government can help Indian companies to do export to foreign countries by doing a 'Easy Exporting Institution' which exporter institution will take every tension to deliver our products in foreign countries. By this Institution, one small businessmen from a village can export to foreign countries. Our Government should also make secure system for every small and big companies because many small companies lost their existence due to big diplomacy of big companies. And this can be done only through strict and hard punishment system. Just one year ago, Google company gave more than 15,000 crores for data information corruption. Such type of punishment provides force to run business with principles.

One big reason for our economical losses is the weak value of money in International market. Our Government should take every little step to strengthen our Rupee. We are now very weak in front of US Dollar and other currencies. Now Indian Government can do anything for the benefit of our country because we have the great power and that is the huge Indian market. Because of this power, foreign countries can obey every condition of our country. One big idea to increase Indian currency value is the vast usage of Indian currency in international transactions. Like Iran Government agreed to take Indian money for oil selling, other country will also agree to do transaction with Indian currency. It is also the perfect time to make our currency international currency. In many area, India should make compulsory transaction of Indian money for foreign companies. India will also give foreign companies tax benefit for using Indian money in international markets. To buy any mineral from India, our Government should make compulsory of US Dollar payments and Indian money payments. To strengthen, our Government can bring Dollar to India and many countries can give us Dollar. China earning huge quantity of US Dollar every year and also reducing Dollar from Chinese treasury to give benefit to its economy. India can exchange Rupee and can bring Dollar from China. Because China also getting benefit from Indian market, it will obviously agree to exchange. But we may face problem by doing 1 Dollar = 1 Rupee but in long term we can get huge benefit from our strong currency like England and USA now getting benefits. But we need to make our Rupee balance because we have to export goods of our country. Because we shall to sell and export Indian manufacturing goods with best price to foreign countries.

Another idea I want to share which can help to India. India can develop a system like COMCASA of USA because India has huge military power and satellite power. India can easily help countries like Srilanka, Bangladesh, Myanmar, Vietnam, Bhutan etc by helping in defence system like

COMCASA. By that India can achieve success in many international diplomacy and international business. I will continue my survey for various solutions and will continue writing in second edition of this book.

Chapter VI: Solution for Educational Problems

To maintain and develop education system, our Government spending a huge amount of money every year. After all educational programme and educational budget, we cannot see any effective social improvement and cannot see any proper syllabus and practical education in our country. I want to compare education with agriculture. If we are spending thousands of rupees to do agriculture and forgetting to spend a little amount of money to do treatment for insects then we are indirectly wasting our money. Similarly, we are wasting thousands of crores in education process by ignoring corruption, undeveloped plans, unpractical education, useless syllabus and negligence in other areas. Because there are rare Government educational institutions which are giving education seriously. In maximum Government educational institutions, we can find bad maintenance and negligence in education. We cannot find any serious survey for running education in schools, colleges and in universities. We can find survey for infrastructure in educational institutions. We can see many movements by Government teachers for better facilities. We cannot find any movement or demand by same teachers to make developmental syllabus, to make useful and practical syllabus and to make better education system. Once they get Government job, then they have no concern for country except their salary.

I am also among the millions of students who suffer for bad education system in our country. when I was doing graduation in a Government college of Odisha, I was facing regular problems. After doing requests, we were getting rarely one honours class in a week and 20 classes in a year and there were three senior faculty of English in that college. Because they are Government employee, they have no problem for any negligence. I even complained against our HOD for not taking any class but as a result I had to face hard words from our HOD and from our Principal. If we start to survey problems in Govt. educational institutions, then we can find uncountable problems and danger negligence of Govt. faculties. We cannot find any punishment for any Govt. faculty. They are doing negligence fearlessly and openly. I am watching same problems in a Govt. autonomous college where I am doing job as a guest faculty of English. Regular faculties are behaving like a Boss with guest faculties and giving most of their duties to them and living like a king. Our Government should give seriousness to finish such type of insects in our Education system. There are huge quantity of qualified students to do job. Therefore, our Government should not hesitate to suspend a lecture for life time with fine who neglect and who doing corruption and there are many qualified students who can take that place easily.

Another big problem in our education system is our education syllabuses. It is a serious and danger problem of our country. We should not take education as a comedy. Now millions of students facing problems to make career after completing education. There are many students who will complete their education very soon. Every year more than one million young people completing their education and starting search for career. Therefore, career is a big problem in India and this problem is increasing every year.

Our education should solve this problem. But we cannot find more than 5% from our syllabus which are useful in real life. Therefore, our Government should take education as a great tool for country making. After completing B. Tech of four years, students are to take minimum 2 year of working experience to do work properly in a company or industry. Here we can say that every student destroying their 4 years and should take direct practical education and should do direct practice to do work in field. They should take basic and fundamental knowledge. Similarly, cannot find any utilitarian education till graduation and above. In this way every +2 pass students wasting 12 years and +3 pass students wasting 15 years in their life. If our syllabuses of schools are giving practical knowledge through stories then our students will obviously get benefit from these educations. We can create interest for programming language through the story of many children who successfully created many video game and other software. We can give them knowledge of various kind of income source through stories. In science part, we can give them knowledge of making various things, knowledge on process of research, knowledge on benefits, knowledge on utilization of various objects in various fields. They should get knowledge through interesting stories or interesting process. In college educations, students should know more practical things of the world. They should study more practical knowledge through which they can get best knowledge on career and on world. Our education should be like that by which one 10th pass student can create his own career and can make research, a +2 pass student can do innovation and can deal very well in business, a +3 pass students can do best job in the field of his education and can earn money by utilize his education. We should give our students the success story of Jeff Bezos, Warren Buffet, Zuckerberg, Ritesh Agarwal, Byju Raveendran etc with their business model knowledge. Students should have complete knowledge on various field of career before 10th class because they will choose their field after 10th class. We cannot ignore even agriculture knowledge which can help more than other knowledge. Arts students are facing much more problems for career because 98% of their education are useless in real or practical world. By making syllabus like above discussed, our Government can secure the career of our students and by which our country will get much more benefit. We should not take syllabus process as little thing because only syllabus system can bring revolution in our country within 5 years.

Our Government should not think that after changing of syllabus, students will not find books. I want to give a great solution that our Government can make PDF format of every book then release those into internet and everyone can download those books from internet freely (without any payment). Here our Government will give public information of book downloading website through advertisement and through other campaign. To prepare such format of books, our Government can give tender to various writers who will make stories and will write books according to order. This total process will take less than two years of time.

To develop research field, our Govt should take some decisions by which people can give priority to research field. Our Government should give life time Penson to innovator and to creative students. Research field should get positive impression from every guardian. I discuss broadly this topic in my 'Solution for Innovation Problem' chapter.

At the end, I would like to give two best solutions for corruption problem and negligence problem in education field. First is the proper use of technology. Our Govt. should open a website for public to complain against any negligence and corruption. A student can at least share the problems of his educational institution, and his/her name cannot show after complain. A student will have to go to his local page and to his/her institution page and then he/she will complain there. Every Government institution will have a page in that website and this thing will help to take action and to survey. Students can give the direct name of neglecting person without fear because this website will not show the name and detail of complainer. Students can upload photo and video as a prove. Second solution is the strict punishment and action against corrupted faculty after complain and after survey. They should be punished, otherwise people will lose believe and will not complain again in that website. If our Government start to take action then every faculty will automatically get information and will do duty properly. Then people will be happy for this. This will be proper democratic system also.